COMMUNITY · CONNECTIONS

?

HOW DO THEY HELP?
GREENPEACE FUND

BY KATIE MARSICO

CHERRY LAKE Publishing

Published in the United States of America by Cherry Lake Publishing
Ann Arbor, Michigan
www.cherrylakepublishing.com

Content Adviser: Rob Fischer, Ph.D., Professor and Director, Master of Nonprofit
Organizations, Jack, Joseph, and Morton Mandel School of Applied Social Sciences,
Case Western Reserve University
Reading Adviser: Marla Conn MS, Ed., Literacy specialist, Read-Ability, Inc.

Photo Credits: © Tinxi/Shutterstock, cover, 1, 13; © FloridaStock/Shutterstock, 5;
© Rich Carey/Shutterstock, 7; © Bettmann/CORBIS, 9; © Steve Morgan / Alamy Stock Photo, 11;
© Michael Wheatley / Alamy Stock Photo, 15; © PhilAugustavo/istock, 17;
© bikeriderlondon/Shutterstock, 19; © Jani Bryson/istock, 21

LIBRARY OF CONGRESS CATALOGING-IN-PUBLICATION DATA
Names: Marsico, Katie, 1980-
Title: Greenpeace Fund / by Katie Marsico.
Description: Ann Arbor, Michigan : Cherry Lake Publishing, [2016] |
Series: Community connections : how do they help? | Audience: K to
   grade 3. | Includes bibliographical references and index.
Identifiers: LCCN 2015048729| ISBN 9781634710497 (hardcover) |
   ISBN 9781634711487 (pdf) | ISBN 9781634712477 (pbk.) |
   ISBN 9781634713467 (ebook)
Subjects: LCSH: Environmental protection—International cooperation—Juvenile
   literature. | Greenpeace Foundation—Juvenile literature.
Classification: LCC TD170.15 .M378 2016 | DDC 363.7/0577—dc23
LC record available at http://lccn.loc.gov/2015048729

Cherry Lake Publishing would like to acknowledge the
work of The Partnership for 21st Century Learning.
Please visit www.p21.org for more information.

Printed in the United States of America
Corporate Graphics
CLFA11

CONTENTS

4 Protecting the Planet

8 From Past to Present

16 Funding Earth's Future

22 Glossary

23 Find Out More

24 Index

24 About the Author

PROTECTING THE PLANET

Polar bears depend on sea ice to survive. Many scientists believe, however, that pollution is causing climate change. As temperatures rise, the polar bears' frozen kingdom slowly melts away.

Luckily, organizations such as Greenpeace Fund exist. This group helps raise awareness about

Polar bear populations were nearly wiped out in the 1800s due to aggressive commercial hunting.

Are you able to guess how much Arctic sea ice has already vanished? In Greenland alone, 10 billion tons of ice have disappeared every year for the past 10 years!

environmental threats. It also helps find solutions to environmental problems.

Greenpeace Fund helps **activists** explore how human actions affect the health of the planet. As a result, people learn more about how pollution, overfishing, and **deforestation** are harming Earth. In addition, they discover new ways of becoming more environmentally responsible. Money from Greenpeace Fund pays for research and educational programs across the globe.

In the rain forest, trees are cut down to make space for houses and farms or to sell as lumber.

THINK!

Think about the many different ways that deforestation harms the environment. How do you think clearing trees changes life for local animals? How about people? Predict how deforestation will impact the planet in the future.

FROM PAST TO PRESENT

Greenpeace Fund is part of a larger global nongovernmental organization known as "Greenpeace, Inc." Canadian activists created Greenpeace in 1971 after learning that the U.S. government was conducting underground **nuclear** testing on Amchitka. This island is located off the Alaskan coast.

Greenpeace got its name from the old fishing boat the organization's founders took to Amchitka.

Can you guess how nuclear testing would trigger a tidal wave? Did you say that blasts from nuclear explosions would make the bottom of the ocean shake? If you did, you'd be right!

Greenpeace founders worried that explosions on Amchitka would harm wildlife and possibly cause a tidal wave.

Members of Greenpeace decided to **protest** the U.S. government's actions by organizing a boat trip to the island. Sailing near a nuclear-testing site was dangerous. Yet activists reasoned that their voyage would force officials to make a choice. If testing continued, officials would either have to tow the Greenpeace boat or publicly risk the crew's safety.

The Greenpeace ships are called: Rainbow Warrior, Arctic Sunrise, and Esperanza.

Look at this photo
of a Greenpeace
protest. What
methods are activists
using to stand up
for the environment?
How is what you
see similar to
what Greenpeace
protesters did
in 1971? How is
it different?

The U.S. Coast Guard stopped the activists before they reached their destination. Still, Greenpeace drew a great deal of public attention to the environmental threat on Amchitka. Ultimately, the U.S. government abandoned its nuclear testing there.

Since 1971, Greenpeace has grown into an international **nonprofit** with more than 2.8 million members. Many of them protect the environment through **lobbying** and peaceful protests.

#IceRide was a global Greenpeace demonstration to help save the Arctic and its wildlife. Protesters biked city streets with balloons!

Learn more about Greenpeace's early efforts. How did activists come up with the name "Greenpeace"? How did they raise money for their first voyage?

13

Activists involved with Greenpeace Fund support environmental research and educational programs. They provide **grants** that help fund Greenpeace's activities in 55 countries, including the United States and Canada. Such large-scale efforts depend on a wide variety of volunteers and paid staff. Some are accountants, fund-raisers, and grant writers. Others are scientists, legal experts, and people who work closely with the media.

There are more than 15,000 volunteers who help Greenpeace each year.

Greenpeace receives all of its financial support from either Greenpeace Fund or private donations. It doesn't seek money from governments or **corporations**. How do you think this policy helps Greenpeace focus on protecting the environment?

15

FUNDING EARTH'S FUTURE

Grants from Greenpeace Fund help pay for different environmental campaigns. For example, they allow activists to research the effects of nuclear testing, deforestation, and overfishing. Money from Greenpeace Fund also supports studies on how toxic, or poisonous, chemicals pollute the land, air, and water.

Helping to keep rivers and streams clean of toxins is just one of the types of projects Greenpeace Fund supports.

RNING
LUTED
ATER
or Drinking
ational Use

OF PUBLIC HEALTH

OF PUBLIC HEALTH

LOOK!

Go online with a parent or teacher. Look for more information about environmental campaigns that depend on the support of Greenpeace Fund. Search for photos and articles about any issues that activists are trying to address in your area!

In all of these cases, Greenpeace Fund encourages activists to think about the future of the planet. Grants fund programming that teaches people about sustainable living. A sustainable lifestyle involves making everyday choices that use up less of Earth's **natural resources**. Sometimes such choices are as simple as buying products from environmentally friendly companies.

Many of the ways we buy and consume food are not good for the environment.

How does shopping for canned tuna fit into sustainable living? Greenpeace Fund supports a great deal of research on companies that sell this product. Why do activists think certain fishing practices are a problem? Do they have any solutions?

19

Greenpeace Fund supports efforts to reveal how various groups impact Earth. Activists hang banners, hold peaceful protests, and publish guides and magazines. They help people make informed decisions and practice sustainable living.

Thanks to Greenpeace Fund, people have a better understanding of environmental problems and are able to find more ways to protect the planet's future.

Greenpeace Fund relies on kids like you to help make a difference today and in the future.

Ready to protect the planet? Create cool recycling containers by decorating cardboard boxes with crayons, markers, glitter, and glue. Place the containers around your home and school. Once they're full, empty them at your local recycling center!

GLOSSARY

activists (AK-tih-vists) people who campaign for social change

corporations (kor-puh-RAY-shuhnz) large businesses

deforestation (dee-for-uh-STAY-shuhn) the act of burning or cutting down all the trees in a certain area

grants (GRANTS) sums of money given by an organization for a particular reason or purpose

lobbying (LAH-bee-ing) seeking to influence lawmakers or public officials on a particular issue

natural resources (NA-chuh-ruhl REE-sors-uhz) materials or substances such as water and forests that occur in nature and are useful to humans

nonprofit (nahn-PRAH-fit) not existing for the main purpose of earning more money than is spent

nuclear (NOO-klee-uhr) related to a powerful form of energy created by activity within atoms

protest (PROH-test) to act in a way that demonstrates disapproval or resistance

FIND OUT MORE

BOOKS

Claus, Matteson. *Animals and Deforestation*. New York: Gareth Stevens Publishing, 2014.

Hawley, Ella. *Exploring Our Impact on the Environment*. New York: PowerKids Press, 2013.

Linde, Barbara. *Pollution*. New York: Gareth Stevens Publishing, 2014.

WEB SITES

Environment Canada—Youth Zone
www.ec.gc.ca/sce-cew/default.asp?lang=En&n=87740C94-1
Check out this site to read more about fun, easy ways to protect the environment!

Greenpeace International—Kids for Forests
www.greenpeace.org/international/en/campaigns/forests/kff/
Visit this page to learn how young people everywhere are fighting deforestation.

INDEX

activists, 6, 12, 16, 18, 20

deforestation, 6, 7, 16

education, 6, 14
environmental problems, 6, 12, 20

Greenpeace Fund
  funding, 15
  history, 8–12
  how it protects the environment, 6, 16–20
  members, 12
  ships, 10–11
  what it does, 4–7
  workers, 14–15

lobbying, 12

natural resources, 18
nuclear testing, 8–10, 12, 16

overfishing, 6, 16, 19

polar bears, 4–5
pollution, 4, 6, 16–17

protests, 10–12, 20

rain forests, 6–7
research, 6, 14, 16, 19

sustainable living, 18–20

ABOUT THE AUTHOR

Katie Marsico is the author of more than 200 children's books. She lives in a suburb of Chicago, Illinois, with her husband and children.